Sold Out for God,

Poetically Speaking

Bob McCluskey

SOLD OUT FOR GOD,
POETICALLY SPEAKING
Copyright © 2016 by Bob McCluskey

All rights reserved. Neither this publication nor any part of this
publication may be reproduced or transmitted in any form or by any
means, electronic or mechanical, including photocopying, recording
or any information storage and retrieval system, without permission
in writing from the author.

Thanks to Sunshine Hills Foursquare Church (6749 120th Street,
Delta, BC V4E 2A7, Phone 604-594-0810, Fax 604-594-6673) for all
of their help and support with my books.

Printed in Canada

ISBN: 978-1-4866-1104-1

Word Alive Press
131 Cordite Road, Winnipeg, MB R3W 1S1
www.wordalivepress.ca

Cataloguing in Publication may be obtained through Library and
Archives Canada

Are We Gods

July 18, 2015

Have you ever wondered, when God looks down
on this rotating sphere of an earth.
Does God ever wonder, "what did I start"
What feelings elicit within God's heart,
such as love, and most probably mirth.

We must remember, God is cognizant of
vast numbers of spheres beyond count.
Our speck of a sphere would be hidden, I fear
in the uncounted billions existing, I hear
in the Milky Way's cloudy amount.

Upon our sphere, gathered busily here,
are billions and billions of men.
Our billions see us as the be-end of all,
we are larger than life, we can never be small,
on perception's deceit, we depend.

So in our turn, are we gods in a way
to the worlds that exist, at our feet.
Only microscopes, could reveal where they went,
but indifferent we are, never benevolent
like our God who loves us, I repeat.

Sweet Relief

July 22, 2015

For beauty, never much cared I,
my heart was oft enticed
but never bared the lie.
The world, at least the world I knew
didst turn around the needs I used
to ever blindly misconstrue
the true reality of you,
until this dead man tasted life.

This waking, not of my design
removed my subtle veil
of rankest ignorance.
Massed foliage surrounding me
burst into brilliant, vibrant green.
The sky, once of a somber hue,
with subterfuge exposed,
became the brightest blue
repentant man has ever seen.

I once was blind but now I see,
God came, God blessed,
God gifted me eternity.
When Jesus Christ, who knew me then
went to the cross, rebellious men
to save, I was chief.

And now, within the heart
of Jesus Christ, I now
and evermore find sweet relief.

Hark, Canst Thou Not Hear

July 20, 2015

Hark, canst thou not hear, rumbling wheels of war
betraying distant unrest. Masses under harangue
rise thru fabricated offences of lies, to justify,
then die, as Satan calls to false rest.

Once more, a tyrant possessed of hell,
    with demonic
power doth entice, to a newer kind of
    world destruct,
power displayed in the sun run amuck,
    and reduced
to the hand of man, then usurped by Satan's plan.

Condensed, refined, cunningly designed,
    bottled hell!
Threatened nuclear retribution
Ok for a while but incessant guile
    ultimately prevailed,
resulting in wide, undisciplined distribution.

Nations marshal before our eyes against Israel!
Zechariah revealed that this is the plague
wherewith God shall smite these nations.
Their flesh shall consume away while they stand!
Their eyes shall consume away in their holes!
Their tongue shall consume away in their mouth!
Aint war grand!

Bob McCluskey

This revelation of atomic destruction compels us,
as we see these events unfolding, to hide.
There be one place only by God's grace, to abide,
that place be Jesus Christ. So quickly, kiss the Son
of God, repent thy sin and invite God's Holy Jesus in
to thy heart, for all eternity be freed from sin.

Thoughts Cascade

July 19, 2015

My thoughts cascade
like leaves from trees.
Feel free my friend,
take one of these
and engage with it.

Some thoughts invest
to elicit intrigue.
Or betimes a thought
might relieve fatigue,
just pray with it.

My thoughts ever fall
quite close to my tree.
none need complain,
every one falls free.
Again and again
it'll comfort thee,
with language plain.

And then at the end
of poetic thought,
may a rhyme become
God's forget-me-not.

To ever intrude
when feelings conclude
with joy in your heart
for an afterthought.

Clandestine Sinner

July 18, 2015

When I see evil
around the world,
and hear the epithets,
thoughtlessly hurled
at my faultless person
in aggravation,
my limp locks
do relentlessly curl
in condemnation.

When they swear at me
don't they understand,
I am the center
of all God planned
when He fashioned man
in the likeness of God.
If they knew me well,
I know they'd repent
at my reprimand
and surely applaud.

What's that you say,
God's dissecting me.

He doth sever my clavicle
just to see,
what dwells within
this heart of mine,
to find I'm a sinner
clandestine.
Oh, woe is me,
I'm no longer blind.
Yea, now I see.

A Poets Life

July 18, 2015

Just resting my old life away,
doth drive my wife berserk.
Idly brooking much delay,
I do this now, most every day,
(I must find gainful work.)

But I am entitled here to be,
this is required each day of me,
for a poet I've become.
Each noonday, off to work I go,
this too, be gainful work, you know.

You've no idea, how much ire
a poem's construction doth require,
it pains me to confess.
I start the day, a decent sort
but by day's end, I must report
my psyche's in a mess.

Subsisting on the kind largesse
of someone up above.
A poet's life doth helpless lie,
dependent in the bye and bye,
on a crust of bread, a coffee cup
and love.

Carnage

July 18, 2015

A thought didst penetrate my reverie,
upsetting my ingrained intent.
Sinful men must die, it doth suggest
in scripture writ of old, and yet
this pains a part of me.

My mind envisions carnage, when
Lord Jesus Christ returns again
and scripture is fulfilled.
Could not God destroy just sin
when Jesus Christ doth enter in.

And so,
back to that resounding thought
I referenced up above.
Could it not, possibly be true
that just the sin in me and you,
might be destroyed by Love.

Might not everyone alive that day,
have all their sin diffused away
by the overpower of God.
Might not everyone with sore intent,
fall on their face and all repent,
as the Sons of God applaud.
God help us Lord!

Iciness Vast
July 15, 2015

In the beginning, if one would have been
witness to iciness vast.
No existence to mark out aeons of time,
no stake in the ground
one could travel around,
no reference point to ever dream
of a God from a nebulous past.

In the midst of eternity under defined,
in a silence redeeming the lie.
A command didst shatter the stygian night,
God's voice proclaimed, "Let there be light".
Then the wonder of God speak
converted the night,
to a brilliantly painted sky.

Next, God commanded and heavens appeared,
a firmament they were called.
With the waters above and the waters below,
when God's voice commands, it has to be so.
Man cannot understand, how a God command
can cause the earth and the heavens to grow.
Man will never know.

Man will never know all God's mysteries,
whilst here on earth he must stay.
Seeing through a glass darkly, inhibits our sight
till that wonderful day we break into God's light.
To know as we are known,
filled with the delight
of Christ, on our glory day.

Gods Serendipity

July 16, 2015

So delicate, so fragile, beauty
drafted by God's patient hand.
Where, at his board was crafted
from the mind of God,
eternal beauty yet unsullied
by the mind of man.
Beauty so resplendent
in a major key
as sky in glory spread.
But beauty also,
destined evermore to be
munificent,
in veiled perceptibility.
Hidden blooms of varied hue
in varied creativity,
concealed from me and you
do live to thrive, denied review
in celebrated serendipity.

Unseen Beauty

July 15, 2015

Beauty in a rose
Exists because
A watchers eye
Didst glimpse it
I suppose
Ere it must die

How rare wouldst
Beauty's dream
Discover
Hidden pleasure
To redeem
Each bloom
Unseen

And yet
God freely grants
These gifts to man
Tho man's
Trammelled thought
Sees naught
Of God's
Extravagance

Futility

July 11, 2015

Futility! The word doth ring with shame,
suggesting all lacks motivation.
What, didst ancient bard proclaim
with scarce enamored adulation,
is in a name.

A bloom adorned with any other appellation
wouldst suffice,
to render our olfactory senses
overwhelmed by floral approbation,
equally as nice.

And so, I humbly do submit to thee
another word, to take its place,
which in due course, wouldst be
quite adequate to then erase
futility's decree.

HOPE! Ah Hope, it's clarion call doth ring,
with one fell swoop, doth circumvent futility,
that beastly thing.
When used with faithful, brave intent,
'twould make futility repent.

HOPE! Ah Hope, eternally doth Hope parade
to reverse discouragement, futility made.
Hope, regally enthroned twixt Faith and Love
by God, restoring mankind from above.
Faith, Hope & Love so perfectly, in Jesus Christ
eternally portrayed.

Rod Of God's Mouth

July 14, 2015

One day anon, the foot of Christ
shall touch upon the mount in Israel.
To usher in, to then begin
the transformation of this earth,
forever paradise from blatant sin.

When the Sword of the Lord is sheathed,
when the rod of His mouth
has destroyed the wicked.
When the will of the Lord has been breathed,
the land shall be as a fold for flocks.

The wolf shall lie with the baby sheep,
and the lion shall feed on straw.
The cow and the bear
shall be friendly there,
fulfilling God's perfect law.

God will joy in His people,
and will rejoice in Jerusalem.
No more will be heard the voice of weeping,
heaven and earth, renewed in His keeping,
the righteous shall dwell in them.

Bob McCluskey

Dream People
July 7, 2015

My mind asleep, doth oft enamor
of the characters, who clamor
through the dreams I dream
bereft of conscious thought.
These dream people, I assure you
would most certainly, soon cure you
of complacently relating
to their ilk, who know them not.
Now this mystery doth elude me,
every night when they intrude, we
seem to be the best of friends
although we have not ever met.
So wherever do they come from,
masquerading to be someone
in my cranium's conundrum
when asleep, to make me fret.
If I could, I would not let them
as I said, I've never met them
they seem so real, its eerie
leaving me this final query.
Who owns that other
vacant head, when they go
somewhere else instead.

Even So, Lord, Come
July 3, 2015

I see them in my mind as on they go
in measured ranks.
Their blood and flesh
Be torn asunder by the treads of tanks.
They cannot think, they cannot know,
theirs not to question why
as on they go, as on they die.

I see their faces then, teeth clenched,
their lives are not their own.
They're only boys,
they're scarcely grown to men
and will not live again, once blood is sown
o'er field and glen, they've never even known,
and all for what.

Some despot ensconced regally somewhere,
is motivated by some evil deep desire
to serve his god, to burn the world with fire,
with not a thought, with not a care
for populations over here or over there.
World armies once again, man must beget,
no option has he, evil must be met.

Our cry Lord Jesus, even so please come,
restore the world to that which thou ordained
would one day soon, forever be reclaimed
by Thee for everyone.
Bind Satan by Thy angel with that
        indestructible chain,
cast him into hell, to burn one thousand years,
cleansing earth of evil...no more tears.

Relationships

July 3, 2015

Who am I
And for that matter
Who are you
I mean within
The constraints
Of much deeper things
Such as how then
Shall we all relate
Through heaven's gate
Amidst the whirl
Of angels wings
How will Jesus
Sort us out
We'll have to learn
I do assume
How we must see
All other people
In the room
Like, me to you
And you to me
We always will be
Quite replete
Without the need
Of food to eat

Or for that matter
Where to sleep
I would assume
We won't
I guess the things
We think we'll need
We'll find out with
the greatest speed
We don't

Relationships 2
July 3, 2015

And furthermore
As I pondered this thought
I thought about clothes
If I looks anything then
Like I now appears
It's incumbent on me
To let no one see
My unrepented arrears
I then thought of shoes
To perambulate me
What would I use
This then directed me
To Exodus 3
Where God said
"Draw not nigh hither
Put off thy shoes
From off thy feet"
So when you and I
Are waiting to be
In the presence of God
Most assuredly we
Must not wear shoes
To be standing around
On Holy Ground

All this thinking
Is quite tiring
Methinks now
I'll be retiring
From these judgements
So profound
And so, goodnight

Sore Silences

July 4, 2015

We don't relate well
To each other
So let's just
Keep it that way
We really have
Nothing to tell
To each other
In other words
Nothing to say
So why would we
Stretch in each other
Credulity, shrinking
At how one relates
Being forced to endure
Painful silences
It's so awkward
Which both of us hates
We act nonchalant
As we painfully flaunt
Our aplomb,
Just to cover our angst
When we finally
Breathlessly, carefully try
To elicit what's hopefully
Finally, goodbye
As we offer to God
Sincere thanks

Breath of Morning

July 2, 2015

Gently, the breath of morning sings
through serrated branches
on silver wings.
A squirrel awakens, chancing
that the cat below yet sleeps.
Then endeavors highway branching
to God's gift of nuts he keeps
for a time like this.

Meanwhile, nesting high in the tree,
when her eggs cracked open
robin mothered three, very hungry chicks.
All day she brings on busy wings,
bugs, spiders, plus other mysterious things
God provides for their wide open, gaping maws.
It's her nature, from God's everlasting laws
for a time like this.

As the earth swings wide, encircling the sun,
summer starts to fade ere winter's begun.
The squirrel's tucked in for his winter soirée,
robin's chicks are fledged, at least two of three.
The cat got one, but God has to be pleased
with creation's encompassing rhapsodies.
God's provision is ever designed to exist
for a time like this.

Our Living Room
July 1, 2015

Most everyone has a
Living Room,
it's the center of our home.
When we tire of life,
of the daily strife,
where we gather
to be alone.

If a room for the living,
there also could be,
one for ranting and raving
to satisfy craving.
Or even for praying,
to hide in for prayer,
maybe Jesus lives there.

Should we call it,
perhaps conversely,
a Dying Room instead.
If we die to self,
we're assured of a place
to meet Jesus in heaven
face to face, by an angel led.

So that dying room
is the place to hie,
for we need to repent
before we die.
That's where Jesus might go
as He waits to bestow
forgiveness, on the penitent.

Just a Cushion

July 4, 2015

You went to high school
And I went to low
Or else I went
To college
And you didn't go
But what doth it matter
We end up the same
Trying hard to keep warm
At the end of our game
If one has lots of money
It mattereth not
Practicing parsimony
Didst fill up thy pot
But to end cold and shaking
So what
You can buy what you want
But your wants are quite bare
All you want is a cushion
To put on your chair
Whilst I have no gold
No desirable sum
I too, just need a cushion
To comfort my bum
So we end up the same
When our race has been run
Mine old frère

Bereft of Me

June 29, 2015

As I navigate the populace,
that over populates this place.
That seeketh evermore to be
abreast of me

Intent on merely getting by,
I blend within an opaque sky
where none may isolate for thee,
a test of me.

With no desire to subjugate
another soul, or to inflate
ambition, displayed just to see
the rest of me.

I winsomely accept invoice
from someone, of a somber voice
and shrouds aplenty, so that he
might vesture me.

Anonymous, without a name
I'll merely leave the way I came.
Unheralded, the world to be
bereft of me.

I Visited My Clinic

June 29, 2015

I visited my clinic on the weekend,
as on each and every weekend
I must do.
My heart requires the treatment
they provide me,
along with many other weakened people who
despair of their condition, which is chronic
and require resuscitate, not just a few.

There's another segment of us at the clinic,
who do complain of feeling rather weak.
There must be another element we're lacking,
are we weakened by insidious back tracking,
something in our makeup's incomplete.

So Pastor Preston didst assess our weak condition,
recognising it was Satan's mass delusion.
Then proceeded to put us all into remission,
by a lovely Holy Spirit Blood transfusion.

We're surrounded in this world
        by weakened people,
who are not aware our clinics e'en exist.
It behooves us to adjure them,
that there is a place to cure them
of the emptiness that veils them, like a mist.

Puny Man
June 27, 2015

Defy God if thou must, Oh puny man,
on what then dost thou trust.
Reveal to me the thrust
of thy prognostication, thy élan,
if thou yet can.

Dost thou truly then,
blank nothingness perceive.
Is thy faith so much elastic
'twould stretch that far, fantastic,
thou couldst not be more unromantic,
if on thyself thou didst believe.

The very essence then of life,
doth it exist.
The life that everywhere appears
from whence cometh it.
A fortuitist accident,
thou wouldst perhaps insist.

But life cannot come from nothing,
God knows that men have tried.
They have dissected to investigate
but no life was resurrected,
mattered not the corpse selected,
only God Divine, may life initiate.

None So Blind

June 26, 2015

Father, please give divine revelation I pray,
as I relate what I sense in our future today.
The key that's unfolding in front of our eyes,
is a hate filled blood-letting by two sects who despise
the beliefs of each other with a hatred intense,
which to our western eyes, does not make any sense.

But our problem, you see, is we tend to forget,
that not too long ago, in our western world yet.
Protestants, Roman Catholics were
        infested with hate,
for each other, so they forthrightly
        burned at the stake
dissenters, who bravely refused to recant
their religious beliefs, and remained adamant.

With hindsight that is cleansed by the
        passage of time,
we can see we were blinded to God's Love Divine.
The Shia believe that they serve the true God,
While the Sunnis believe they are
        led by God's truth.
Each burns, cruelly slaughters,
        and then they applaud
as each seeks to control man's existence, forsooth.

I now see that we, in the vast Christian west,
over decades now past, really gave it our best
to convert all these billions,
        to change them enmasse,
but we did not consider the time that must pass
even hundreds of years ere
        these billions could change
not one or two years, to their lives rearrange.

The consequence of our meddling,
        I'm sorry to say,
Gave rise to a force that's pre-eminent today.
They are gathering strength in the
        inflamed Middle East
and their avowed hatred of Israel,
        I believe is the least
of our troubles because their clear stated fate
is to convert the whole world
        by a strong Caliphate.

The last days God revealed, have already begun,
but we won't bring God's kingdom to earth
        with the gun.
God revealed if we pray, He'll one day intercede
and bring cleansing to conquer
        all bloodshed and greed.
So our future depends, to which God we relate,
Jesus Love will consume man's rebellion and hate.

Over and Out

June 25, 2015

Cluskey 1 to God
Ready for take-off
God to Cluskey 1
Clear for take-off
Cluskey 1 to tower (God)
Alpha Bravo Charlie
Tower to Cluskey 1
Weather is mixed
Have a good life
Cluskey 1 to tower
ABC. clear skies ahead
Tower to Cluskey 1
Contact tower each day
Along life's way
Alpha, Bravo, Charlie
Roger, Over

Years Later

Cluskey 1 to tower
Mayday, mayday
I've run out of gas
At end of my flight
Permission to land
As I fade into night

Bob McCluskey

I can talk to you Jesus
I don't have to shout
Alpha Bravo Charlie
Over and out

Thoughts For Susanne

June 27, 2015

All this, which
in this life
participates,
is for you,
for me,
for all.
So transient,
a mere brief
preparation
for eternity
to come,
much loftier
in station.
God awaits
the call,
yet 'tis God,
man's final
transference
initiates.

Mystic Earth

June 23, 2015

Mystic earth that shaped the rose
made too, the weed that choked it.
A mystery, one wouldst propose
as to what or who evoked it.

Creation of such beauty speeds
great joy to the beholder.
One wonders how insatiable weeds
increasingly grow bolder.

This seemeth to perceptive eyes
great evil understated.
Against God's splendour, to despise
sweet beauty God created.

Every gardener thus should know
they labor in God's grace.
Those roses, rooted deep below
flaunt Satan to his face.

Pious Disguise

June 22, 2015

A man proclaimed that God was dead,
in measured speech, pervasive.
They placed a crown upon his head,
his proclamation then was read,
in truth, 'twas quite persuasive.
Professing himself to be wise,
he filled the hearts of doubters,
who were persuaded to despise
God's truth, to aptly ostracize
God's Christian down and outers.

Another man, with great élan
proclaimed God yet existed.
The proof he said, was plain to see,
if God were dead, man could not be,
you must engage your trust in me
he adamantly insisted.
In Col.1:17 God revealed to man
so clear for those with eyes to see,
That, By God All Things Consisted.

The rabble rousers then engaged
to be what rabble rousers be.
They covered their intent with lies,
And then to everyone's surprise
they set a killer free.

Bob McCluskey

Concealed behind pious disguise,
they turned now to this miscreant.
After beating our dissenter well,
they failed to get him to recant
and nailed Christ to a tree.

Our Importance
June 20, 2015

This world existeth long without me,
did it miss me, I wouldst know.
I rather think it didst resist me,
but I really do not know.

And now that I'm at last existing,
along with also, all of you.
Something in my mind's persisting,
I am making much ado

about nothing, source of purpose
lieth not with you or me.
God has a goal, and deigned to use us
to achieve His victory.

Consequently, my importance,
for that matter, also yours.
Lie principally in our acceptance
of Christ Jesus' overtures.

Hallelujah, Christ be Savior
of the spirit's of all men.
Non exempt for sin behavior,
but beloved by Jesus, when
they penitently nurture Him.

Bob McCluskey

Thoughts Come & Go

June 20, 2015

Thoughts come, thoughts go
One knoweth not the source
The brain is wired to be inspired
By any vagrant word of course
If discernible, the eye would see
An intermittent cranial glow
When word meets word
Silent, unheard, to show
A poem's birthing, petulant
Rehearsing get-away ere
Poet knows its purposing
One's mind doth grasp
At thought's suppress
No time to ask
Or e'en express, intent
Poets carelessly allow
These thoughts to stray
They have somehow, a way
Of bringing one to task
By stealing silently away
Perhaps somewhere to bask
In solitude, then launch
To taunt again another day
Alas

Welcome Home

June 17, 2015

Have you ever wondered why you are here,
or for that matter, the other seven billion.
Like, what difference would it make, I'm asking
if the current seven billion didst never appear,
I mean, beyond the obvious things we leave
on the face of the earth, like our shallow scratching,
would the world be any better or be any worse.
I rather imagine the world would get along fine
if man never appeared to create the pollution.
The earth would certainly have clean air sublime,
and there would then not be the need for solution.
The only loss that to my mind would be missed,
might possibly be the mystery of things intangible.
Which, if they were absent or if they were here
would make no physical difference imaginable,
like love or forgiveness or mercy or fear,
they could not exist anyway since no lovers exist.
But then, what would God do with only one Son,
God has so much love He just has to have lovers.
Ah! So now I have the answer to the question above!
God had to have mankind made in His image,
on whom He could pour out all of His pent up love,
so much love that His sons might soon
    number ten billion.

God patently awaits all these billions with
     arms open wide
to embrace them, to love them,
     to welcome them home
to God's Only Begotten Son Jesus Christ at His side.
Welcome Home!

Virtual Reality

June 16, 2015

I see manifest in young men today
a boredom, a need for action.
They see action, excitement as a way
to get into the battle, into the fray,
the roadway to satisfaction.

The horror of war does not really exist,
they see war as exciting, but here's the twist,
They can now go to war on their monitor,
at no risk to themselves, what a lovely war,
and it seems just as real as they wished.

So the need stays alive, they can nurture that drive,
'till one day there could be a real war.
They won't turn that war off when they go to bed,
it won't be on a screen to be fought in their head,
tyrants think that's what young men are for.

It's happening now, God's word says that's the plan,
the tyrants are girding for war.
They believe they can set half the world on fire,
and still win in a war feeding Satan's desire
to kill each God created man.

Our Love

June 15, 2015

Our love,
my love for you,
your love for me,
with age assures.
Love of the heart,
my heart and yours.
Not of the flesh
but ephemeral,
a gift from God
having substance
not at all,
but having
lasting loveliness
that evermore endures.
Love fills
the empty hours
when separation unifies,
when hearts endear
by feelings
like lovely flowers.
When sensitivity
to empathy
becomes the norm,
and we see
without eyes.

I Met a Man

June 15, 2015

I met a man the other day,
jus' puttin' up with life.
Like me, he'd fathered children,
recently he'd lost his wife.

I asked him where he's goin',
he said, retirement I guess.
I knew he had no way o' knowin'
that his life was in a mess.

I asked him if he'd thought about
that black impending wall
that faced him when life ended,
had he thought of it all.

He said he didn't like to
'cause it always made him sad.
I said I understood, then gave him
news that made him glad.

I told him how Christ Jesus died
to save a man like him.
That if he would ask forgiveness,
Christ would wash away his sin.

Bob McCluskey

He said yes, he wanted Jesus,
prayed with me, the sinners prayer.
And now, when I reach heaven
that old man will meet me there.

Angels Glow

June 14, 2015

Angels exist, God's Word says so,
also, many first person accounts.
Since this be so, I would sure like to know
if they'll be here for me, when it counts.

Or have angels been with me already,
to save me from some tragedy.
Without my suspect, have they
    salvaged my neck
so that I could continue to be.

We have entertained angels, unawares,
I remember I read in God's Book.
Its somewhere near the back, if anyone cares,
or it was there the last time I looked.

So the angels can come, look exactly like one
of us folk, who inhabit this sphere.
I would love one to say, in an angelic way,
nice to meet you, so glad to be here.

Take a look at my face, see the glow
    that's in place
that's what happens, when staying with God.
Since I just came from there,
    there's a glow everywhere,
that's why angels do always applaud.

Bob McCluskey

Now I know you'll be glad, to hear
    from Mom and Dad,
they asked me to bring you their love.
But I now have to go, I must leave here below
to replenish my glow, up above.

And It Was God

June 13, 2015

He strained to mount the highest crag,
success seemed not to be.
Just when he felt his courage flag,
some power assured a victory,
and it was God.

The cancer strove to overcome
her weakening estate.
Just when she felt the end was nigh,
she cried to God, a peace came by.
Her strength returned, 'twas not too late,
and it was God.

A soldier lay on burning sand,
his life didst seep away.
With failing strength he raised his hand,
and cried to God to help him stand.
He found he was restored that day,
and it was God.

So many times when it was God,
and miracles occurred.
Man chose to think from natural cause,
whilst God loves on without a pause,
and it was God.

God does not bless us for reward,
God loves without conditions.
Satan waits to use the sword,
his hatred on mankind is poured.
Men now reject his superstitions,
and it was God.

My Rocking Chair

June 13, 2015

Why must it be,
this subtle transformation,
from youth
with all its liveliness displayed.
With scarce discerned
daily disintegration,
to our slow accept
of livings grand degrade.

This unwelcome blight's
unfairly thrust upon us,
as we blithely navigate
life's devious winde.
Without awareness,
this weakening has drawn us,
to the rocking chairs
our grannies left behind.

But I'm really not
expressing dissatisfaction,
I kinda like the pace
if truth were known.
That rocking chair's become
a grand attraction,
to comfort me
till Jesus takes me home.

And So Life Goes

June 12, 2015

We're born, we live, we celebrate,
with fellow travellers, relate.
Some we might like, whilst others hate,
and so life goes.

When I say hate, its 'cause it rhymes.
Much nicer words, I speculate,
most surely wouldst suffice to tell
this story to you just as well,
but this aint prose.

So to continue, may I say,
we go thru life, along the way
we take a wife, or else we may
avoid that strife, to just decay
the cowardly way.

But life's frustration, is not why
I write to thee today.
God opened up my blinded eye,
to show me Jesus Christ is my
true Savior, He's the only way
to live, and not to die.

Sweet Summer Morn

June 10, 2015

Sweet summer morn, a garden born
in seeming natural casualness.
Where insects one can scarcely see,
grace blooms so acrobatically.

So where'd they come from, who designed
their little heads and their small behinds?
The whole package, small as the head of a pin,
but hearts and muscles lie hid within.

With little wings that go like mad,
and legs one wouldn't know they had.
With something trailing out behind,
when missing, they don't seem to mind.

They seem to stay around a time,
a month or two mayhap.
Then the next ten months, they seem to resign
for a rather lengthy nap.

What do they do whilst out of sight,
surely they don't just sleep.
I rather suspect, they're making more specks
in their castles, 'way down deep.

But faithful they be, come July we'll see
them return with all of their brood.
So we know while away, they were making hay,
but we mustn't become too lewd.

Blessed Are The

June 9, 2015

"Blessed are the poor in spirit",
but how can our spirit be poor.
Are we humbled inside when we hear it,
I never could be quite sure.

"Blessed are they that mourn",
folks do a whole lot o' that.
Some seem to mourn from the day they're born,
expectations stay lowly and flat.

"Blessed are the meek" does that mean mild,
must we go thru life like a little child.
Do they come to the end with nothing defiled,
after turning the other cheek.

"Blessed are they that hunger",
God did not mean hunger for food.
God said hunger must be for righteousness,
Not for stomachs to protrude.

Blessed, the merciful, rewarded in kind,
they help Christians who fall into sin.
Otherwise they'd resemble blind leading the blind,
a dangerous place to be in.

Bob McCluskey

This must now be the end, for I've run out or room,
we'll continue another time.
Jesus gave us more teaching; we'll get to it soon,
I just have to prepare more rhyme.

God Bless Heroes

June 9, 2015

Heroic be the effort made,
the momentary loss of sense.
There went the heroes, unafraid
to charge the lofty hill, entrenched.

When men throw caution to the wind
spontaneously, with no recourse.
No opportunity to rescind,
the choice is made, its death or worse.

Where went the instinct to survive,
when in that moment madness reigned.
No thought of coming out alive,
whilst sensibly, the rest remained.

Most heroes lie enthroned in graves
whilst we survive, our lives intact.
Where caution rules, survival saves,
we counted cost before we'd act.

But heroes gave their lives for me,
without their courage, all was lost.
They paid the price to keep us free,
to hell with fear, they paid the cost.

God bless the heroes!

Thy Beauty Fair

June 8, 2015

My eye didst fall
On thy beauty fair
But when I reached out
You were not there
Perhaps thou espied
My ugly side
Bathed ever in greed
And covered in pride
But if thou wouldst return
And look again
On my other side
Thou wouldst remain
For my other side
By Jesus' blood
Is cleansed from sin
From the filth and mud
That greed and pride
Had covered me in
You now would see
My sugar and spice
I'd reach out again
And in a trice
You'd desire to stay
With my side that's nice
For another day

Does Man Need God
June 8, 2015

Man is supreme!
What need hath he of a god to see
himself as free.

Doth man not freely demonstrate
his own creative aptitude!
Why needest he a god to make
his spirit free, his heart relate
it's own creative mystery.

And yet, and yet, what must there be
beyond the limitations, he
is subject to when senses wane,
when all he used to trust became
a mystery.

When soon, if not tomorrow, when,
another morrow sooner then.
The blackness he anticipates
will fade to white, he'll see the gates
awaiting him.

And so, truth then will have its day,
with consequences untoward.
This scenario need never be,
a lovely kiss, and not the sword
wouldst greet him if he would receive
Christ Jesus now, to just believe
God's Word.

God Created Life

June 7, 2015

1 God created life
But ere life could begin
Man created death
Death now becometh him
For God suffered reject
When God extended man
The precious gift of life
But what did God expect
From choice bestowed
When God gave man a wife
Satan's venom flowed
We are a sorry lot
Man now so profligate
From sin that Adam bought
Cometh greed and lust and hate

11 But God did not despair
His plan fared well and true
There'd be no harvest there
True love could not ensue
If man had not free will
That's how God rescued you
Christ Jesus, who is God
Hung on that cross until
The blood He shed
Prevailed instead
Of sin, and ever will

Bob McCluskey

So choose you wisely friend
Your will is all your own
No use to just pretend
Don't wait until
You leave this earth
Salvation will have flown

Communication Consternation

Communication flies on high
The air to fill
Communication tells us why
The senses will
Or why those thoughts distill
To ever upward fly

Man seeketh man aloft, invisibly
His word be hard or soft
Its purpose is to tell what he
Has purposed, what the thought would be
To others, in the words that he
Didst send aloft

If then the passaging were seen, concrete
In simultaneous messaging on high
Effecting then their passaging with wings, not feet
A billion at a time in traffic dense
Flying thru each other never indicating whence
Or where the messaging doth fly

How doth the messaging always reach the one
For whom it is intended instantly

Bob McCluskey

As I labor on this question, would it not be fun
If hand from heaven reacheth down to redirect
The questions to some other destination casually
A destination that the hand from heaven
    would select
Oh Glory Be

Jesus Died For You

June 4, 2015

How unsettling, the news,
presented in such graphic, sad detail.
Repeatedly, gross horror sadly spews
from our T.V. box, our senses to assail.

Why do I watch the damned thing anyway,
I'm elderly, that's just what old men do.
The young could not care less, or so they say,
which category includes all of you.

In any case, we'll find out soon enough,
these graphic slaughters manifest worldwide.
150 people sheltered in the station from the storm,
gas pumps massively exploded, so 150 people died.

The horror of their burning, surely strikes
        a tender chord,
but we're blindly unaware of what's to come.
To be absent from the body's to be present
        with the Lord,
a Godly judgement now awaiteth every one.

That is the greatest horror, men with hearts
        so unprepared,
cannot go back to rearrange their fate.

Each man's choice forever stated, to the world
        so underrated,
as they cry out in God's judgement,
        too late Oh God, too late.

If you say you don't believe it, that is
        your prerogative,
we have free choice, but what if the Bible's true.
God calls us to believe Him, in the Bible
        to receive Him,
Jesus died not just for us, He died for you.

Oh God, How I Hate War!

June 2, 2015

Oh God, how I hate war!
There's a foreboding hovering
right now in the air,
doesn't anyone care, anymore.

Whatever on earth is war for, all the pain,
all the sabres are rattling again.
Young men in their prime
will be slaughtered enmasse, one more time.

No one wins, in their sins young men die
for some tyrant's evil or greed.
Some tyrant's prideful, unfulfilled need,
while bewildered, we all wonder why.

The Bible declares God is love!
I wonder, what doth God think,
seeing men on war's brink,
looking down on mankind from above.

Satan grins with great evil delight,
as he fills some tyrant's heart with hate.
Who then creates a strange God,
masses rush to applaud, imitate.

Young men then all march to their doom,
some not having made peace with the Lord.
Satan welcomes them in, he has room
in his Satanic ward.

Please intercede in our need, precious Lord,
bring an end to this evil flood.
That's why You shed your sinless blood,
to bring all men to Godly accord.
Oh God, how I hate war!

Money or Love

June 6, 2015

What stirreth thy hunger, money or love,
which couldst thee not e'er do without.
Wouldst money suffice, in the place of a wife
who might love thee with never a doubt.

You could buy lots of kisses, from agreeable misses,
they would probably come cheap enough.
But you never would know, if it's you or your dough,
you know how some girls love that stuff.

Or wouldst thou demand her sweet love
    out of hand,
wouldst thou treasure true love, like pure gold.
Wouldst thou e'er pay the cost tho
    thy fortune be lost,
if her heart in thy hands thou couldst hold.

Christ invested His Love when He came from above,
and nailed all our sin to that tree.
He didst treasure love true, when He recovered you
from your sin, as He recovered me.

Where Lie the Hearts

June 1, 2015

Where lie the hearts that ever seek
for goodness in the souls of men.
To stand in Canada the free
for righteousness to cover them.

Where lie the hearts to ever love,
to ever turn the other cheek.
To worship Jesus Christ above
deception, yet be ever meek.

Where lie the valiant, ever strong
to stand against the evil day.
Who stride amongst us, who belong
to those who revel in the fray.

They're born again, these Godly men
who count the cost yet do not faint.
Tho truth requireth each of them
to trust, avoiding evil taint.

Who may not thrill to accolade
bestowed on some less worthy one.
But will hear Jesus on that day,
say to them in His lovely way,
"Well Done!"

Airborne Seeds

May 29, 2015

Spring zephyrs wafting softly o'er,
as quietly at rest I lay.
Bring fluffy floating seeds to fore,
seemingly aloft at play.

What brings thee to my rapt attent,
unconsciously, didst query I.
Oblivious, that careless intervent,
couldst apprehend their passing by.

What's that? No, no, this cannot be,
imagination doth transfix.
Airborne seeds can't talk to me,
minds comprehension playeth tricks.

But did I not again o'erhear
a squeaky little voice assert.
Hey, hey! Ho ho! I'm in the clear,
Surprise! Surprise, it didn't hurt.

I'm off! I'm off to see the world,
whilst thou lie slothily abed.
Into vast open space I'm hurled,
to places where thou canst not tread.

With any luck, yon wind should bring
me to a bed of nurtured earth.
Into which I'll stick my head,
a great big tree, one day I'll birth.

Ho! Ho! Hi! Hi! I'm off....Goodbye.

God's Design

May 29, 2015

When we look into heaven
We look back in time
When we look on a flower
We see God's design
When we look on a baby
A miracle doth birth
Do you not think that maybe
God visited earth
When a man holds a woman
From whence doth love come
God is love, which is scripture
Sent for everyone
You can't see it, can't taste it
Can't know how it's made
But life lived without love
Is an empty charade

Earthquake

May 30, 2015

A very strong 8.5 earthquake struck,
right off the coast of Japan.
Because it was deep, 370 miles,
it did little damage to man.

But it was strongly felt all over Japan,
is God warning man to repent.
Is God doing all that He possibly can,
to spare us, is that what it meant.

God will not always strive with man,
God, please waken the whole human race.
All over the world, not only Japan,
cause man's pride to fall on its face.

Right under our coast, a fault line lies,
please God, before it's too late.
Pour out thy Spirit to open blind eyes,
that we not suffer a sinner's fate.

God, you did it before when revival came,
revealing sin to repentant man's heart.
Jesus Christ is our hope, only one precious Name
for revival, please God let it start.

Why Sin

May 31, 2015

Why are we tempted by sin
Why do we look when we know it's wrong
Why do we even begin
Why does our heart quicken inside
When forbidden fruit is presented
Why do we not suffer instant disdain
For the sin with which we are tempted again
When we know our conscience will suffer pain
To our heart, no longer contented

The apostle Paul recognised it all when he said
For what I would, that do I not
But what I hate, that do I. Oh wretched man
    that I am
Who shall deliver me from the body of this death
The love of Christ, for in all these things
We are more than conquerors through Him
    that loved us
And so to be carnally minded is death
But to be spiritually minded is life and peace
Choose Christ

Lifelong Friend

October 11, 2014

If one would win, another has to lose!
The heart of sensitivity
doth choose, to offer to the other
with the losing, like a brother,
a helping of his choosing
that would succor in the losing,
while not suffering excusing
faulty views.

This expense of small stipend,
would avail him in the end
of someone to betide him,
when false enemies deride him,
to then bravely stand beside him
as on thru life he wend.
I refer of course to someone
who in life would then become one
of the treasures life provide him,
in a word, a lifelong friend.

There's Room At the Cross For You

May 28, 2015

Man moves over the earth
With multitudinous intent
God has a purpose, a plan
Expounded quite clearly for all
In the event man might care to look
In the Bible, His book
But each moving dot
On the face of the earth
In a mass of multiplied billions
Of squirming, serpentine dots
Indiscernible individually to man
But clearly discernible to God
Has a will and purpose of its own, so averse
God knows and loves and indeed died
For each indifferent, self centered dot
God in fact, created each dot in His own likeness
In the image of God, created He them
For His pleasure created He them
But they take no pleasure in God or worse
Until!...Until!...Until!!!...A crashing crescendo
Of momentous revelation
Opens deaf ears and unscales blind eyes
To reveal earth shaking Truth! GOD IS REAL!!!!!

This cannot be, but it is, it is, Hallelujah
GOD IS REAL.....God came...Yes God came
To earth two thousand years ago
To salvage lost man, billions of dots
Crawling all over the earth would be lost
If Jesus Christ had not paid for their sin
When He gave Himself to the cross
And shed the only agent that could cleans
Those billions of dots...The Blood of Christ
Presented to the Father by the Holy Spirit
To evermore be available to save souls
My soul! Your soul! Every soul!
For there's room at the cross for you
Tho those dots have now come
To the cross, every one
There's still room at the cross for you

Ravages of Time

May 21, 2015

Alas, the ravages of time
distills the able bodied man,
to just the essence of the wine
that manifested in those days
when all the world was thine.
When light of foot and fair of face,
life's challenges were met.

No longer harnessed to the needs
required of him anon.
His heart within to fortune win, now bleeds
tears of inadequacy.
He cannot now perform to be
the one to fill the office he
fulfilled, those days are gone.

Now one by one, resources he
in days gone by resounded,
were simple chores, required no thought
more daring ones with danger fraught
he leapt into the fray and fought.
He was the go to guy to see,
conflicting problems he would easily best.

And so doth end, the curtain's fall.
He just pretends to answer call,
but sits back down, he's seen it all
before.

Beauty's Lovely Glow

September 27, 2014

Our balcony doth overlook
ocean's entrancing view.
Not lovelier though, in any book
my dear, than you.

For blessing, I might thou embrace,
whilst all that I behold.
Compares not with thy lovely face,
this vast enfold.

But loveliness takes many forms,
of which thou art but one.
The ocean, throughout calm or storm's
entranced, since time's begun.

Whilst beauty of the rarer kind,
displayed within thy gaze.
Doth grace us for a briefer time,
moths pinned within thy blaze.

And so, throughout this briefest span
of beauty's lovely glow.
I revel, as wouldst any man
till time says, we must go.

Life's Portion Flies

September 27, 2014

Ah life, so unaware are we,
as vital passage flies.
Each portion of our life, that we
assign as dreams, romantically,
e'er life's deception dies.

And so we find a path in life,
believed to be our will.
We weather all the storms and strife,
perhaps we even find a wife, until
life's portion flies.

So there we stand, so unaware
of passaging of time.
But staring into blackness, where
the unknown lingers, lurking there
obscuring the Divine.

Awake! Awake! Thou sleepest late,
there yet availeth time.
God's glorious salvation sweet,
awaiteth in the dark, to meet
thine end of time.

Crime on Television

October 1, 2014

Why is crime glorified on our colored T.V.,
life does have enough crime, already.
What is it in us that seeks ever, a thrill,
watching mugging, a rape or a blood thirsty kill
on our couch, holding beverages steady.

Is our life so mundane that we love to watch pain,
acted out with a splash of red paint.
All lined up in the living room, feeling so bored,
smugly feeling that Jesus would be in accord,
which He aint.

Isn't life bad enough, it can get kinda rough
in real life, without help from the tube.
Hospitals are nearby with real life on display,
you can visit, see pain, and you don't have to pay,
although that might seem, so very rude.

I am rather afraid, that my little tirade
sounds self righteous, although it is not.
I assure you my taste in T.V. is refined,
just the news, scientific, with views of that kind,
though news also degrades now, a lot.

Bob McCluskey

Life's Bitter Pill

October 10, 2014

Bitterest of all pills, the one
that bringeth truth to light.
Our road thru life when once begun,
that riseth t'ward life's setting sun,
seems destined to delight.

And so we strive thru life's constraints,
unmindful of the course
laid out for us, by circumstance
as steps, in our ongoing dance
of joy or of remorse.

Long years ago, the road in place
divided into two.
We chose the left as on we race,
the right, didst other life embrace,
a life we never knew.

We knew not then, nor will we when
our end of road is sealed.
God's mercy hideth this from man,
we know not now, nor ever can,
what might have been revealed.

Clock Within

October 10, 2014

The clock contained within
Each soul endowed with life
Seems unrestrained by sin
Tho shortened some by strife
Some mainspring must require
A winding now and then
Else clock would soon expire
With no warning as to when

When doth winding then occur
When we're asleep, maybe
To be specific, I demur
Having never waked to see
And whereat is the key
Also, where doth it insert
It could be someplace maybe
That could cause a sleeper hurt

Is that why I wake sometimes
With a surly disposition
I always thought it was the clime
Or an awkward sleep position
But they mustn't lose devotion
Else my mainspring might run down
I'd then function in slow motion
Like that television clown

I don't know when they renew me
I think sometimes they forget
Energy then goes right thru me
Really puts me in a sweat
What if they don't ever wind me
I'd lie motionless in bed
Maybe that's how they would find me
On the day they find me dead

In God's Shadow

October 13, 2014

A minister assumes a great burden,
when a pastoral office he fills.
Not like a worldly position
of driver or clerk or physician
who healeth our physical ills.

But is called to step into the shadow
of the God of creation, times three.
Who really is one,
tho we've scarcely begun
to envision who Jesus might be.

Oh, we know in our heads from the bible,
everything about God that we see.
Some who put it together are liable,
to believe it is quite justifiable,
to sever God up into three.

So, a pastor comes under God's shadow,
to shepherd God's sheep, with restraint.
He must teach all, God's truth,
focusing on the youth,
and must deal with each bleating complaint.

Bob McCluskey

These souls he must keep from false teaching,
and must constantly be on his guard.
Bringing truth to the flock,
disregarding the clock
to expose each demonic canard.

He will give an account of his service,
on the day God doth reckon his sin.
Ever destined to be
for the flock, you and me,
God's servant, to shepherd us in.

Who Can Know God's Plan

October 15, 2014

Far away, ensconced on the board of a church,
a middle aged man once served God.
Content with life, a lovely wife,
where they sent their pastor abroad.

This was an annual event, their pastor went
on a preaching exchange, afar.
To many pulpits across the land,
usually just a one day stand,
and he went by plane, not car.

He preached one day far from home,
three thousand miles at least.
In another church, it was prearranged,
no theatrics, he never changed,
but he tendered a spiritual feast.

The altar call the man's pastor gave,
received an excited response.
From a woman who rushed
and would not be denied,
she fell on her knees and cried and cried,
the assembly was awed and hushed.

Her husband and family were overjoyed
at the permanent change in her life.
Thirty years later he passed away,
the other man also lost his wife.
In order to join his children there
he moved three thousand miles
and joined their church.

Of all the churches he could have joined,
she was there.
After time had healed, the Lord revealed
His plan to bring them together.
Thirty five years earlier, God sent
the man's pastor
to prepare her for the day, he would
come and ask her
to marry him, ere they put two and
two together
and discovered God's ancient plan
and His loving care.

Free Air

October 15, 2014

Existence is a nebulous affair!
Into life's reality we come
to fight for air,
requiring yet of course
that we must share.

And sharing then, we trust
there is enough for all.
We respiratory ones who are but dust,
do answer breathing's call
with effortless adjust.

Water on the other hand
is parcelled out to mankind for a fee.
Directed to our metered pipes,
tho God provided it for free
its latterly, just sold to you and me.

I'm certain men have tried
to find a way to parcel up the air.
I'm sure for many sleepless nights,
the prospect fashioned them delights
of air control, to mankind's great despair.

But air control they could not do.
I'm sure it drives them to frustration.
Air comes from God to me and you
Thus filling greedy hearts with consternation,
as we freely breathe each breath of air anew.

Free From Intelecture

September 25, 2014

This life I live but briefly,
seemeth ever to suspend.
I who contend, seemeth chiefly
most important, I pretend.

That's how it ever seemeth,
as I blindly forage on.
Tho I am the one who dreameth,
ignorantly, all along.

But a lifetime of conjecture,
hath conveyed me to the truth.
I broke free from intelecture,
into Love of Christ, forsooth.

For here didst I discover
scripture stating, God is Love.
God Jehovah, there's no other,
hell below or heav'n above.

Who contendeth my departing
in my ignorance, for hell.
Just in time, I lay there smarting,
but recovered very well.

Bob McCluskey

Overjoyed to be selected,
much more trouble tho, for God.
Ever blessed to be elected,
as God's angels all applaud.

Our Autumn Cruise

September 26, 2014

Together Agnes Mary, you and I,
from northern clime to ocean's ebbing tide.
Entranced by swelling sea and sunny sky,
our hearts united, over ocean wide.

With glance upraised, we then beheld aloft,
our ship's unencumbered bow.
Spread out before us, as envisioned oft,
awaiting as if welcoming, somehow.

Overcoming our ship ladder's reckless care,
we mounted foredeck poised, with great élan.
With steady seamen's unaccustomed flair,
we viewed the sea as only lovers can.

Hearts resting now as side by side, content,
we entered shipboard cabins that await.
Immediate, our hearts with love cement,
in everlast surrender to sweet fate.

Safely anchored 'gainst the surging tide,
Captain Saunders, valiant at the helm.
Aboard her ship where she doth now reside,
her flying bridge surveying ocean realm.

Bob McCluskey

With beaming sun's unseasonable largesse,
we drift thru our allotted span of days.
Our seaside flat is shipshape, we confess,
tho we must leave, we'll have our cruise, always.

Am I Solomon

September 18, 2014

Why did God permit the Holocaust?
Don't ask! It's a nerve that you touch!
Why did such a scheme
shatter every man's dream?
Am I Solomon!... You ask me too much.

Why did millions of God's chosen people,
The babies! The children! The old!
March with hands in the air
to the cattle cars where
they en mass went to gas chambers cold!

I said millions! Have you ever seen millions,
a million spreads far, very far!
But six million when spread
horizontally, dead,
leaves mind's cognisance wildly ajar.

So my question was, why did it happen,
was each captor an unfeeling brute?
Did he then go away
to his children each day,
after bathing, to conscience reboot.

Sure, I know there were Nazi fanatics,
but their numbers were not really many.
All the rest of the uniforms just covered men
who treasured their own children waiting,
     but then
every day killed kids, three-for-a-penny.

When war came to an end, did they try to defend
flow of Jewish blood from guilty hands.
Did they lie, did they try, did their God justify,
or did conscience prevail, did they just want to die,
did they have to obey those commands.

I can't answer at all, only God can,
even Solomon was never that wise.
As my mission departs, thank God He
     searches hearts,
were these some He might yet circumcise.

True Security

September 14, 2014

Tis hard in life to feel another's pain,
to stand beside the one who suffered loss
of hard won gain.
We say we care, we utter words of consolation,
expressing our consideration, to assuage
the emptiness away.

Job too had comforters, who came to say
Job was his own misfortunes author,
by the way.
With friends like those to entertain,
Job needed no false enemies, engaging
guilt that day.

But if thy love be ever tried and true,
to family, mayhap yet a son or daughter who
doth grieve anew.
Pain they feel, begins so subtly now to steal
Into thy consciousness, to somehow feel
It's you.

As reality of tenuous security in the world,
of floods and fires, of wartime threats
come crashing in.
A heavy sadness spread like cancer over me,
and rightly so, there's no way now that I could see
to win.

Bob McCluskey

My Godly wife's concern for me,
    prompted her to pray
that God would take my heaviness away,
recover me.
On Sunday next at breakfast as I wracked my brain,
a sudden revelation from our faithful God
    then came
and made me free.

God revealed my discontent was based on
    false foundation,
Lord Jesus Christ, and only He, could be
    for all eternity
the only true security, I've got.
The world, things I possessed were dross
    and mattered not,
two seconds in eternity and all these things
    would ever be
forgot.

Jesus Christ, Messiah

September 13, 2014

The die is cast. Look North! Look East!
those columns of dust attest.
The minions of hate release, release,
the weapons of war that express it best,
God knows the beginning and end.

Oh, the words are soft, but intent is hard
from the Emperor in the business suit.
With heartfelt desire to never retire,
with words of a saint, but heart of a brute
to restore empire.

As he plans ahead for the living dead,
integrating with Israel's foes.
He currently tries to gather allies
from the list each Bible reader knows,
and God decrees.

Allies who surround God's Jerusalem
with slavish, evil intent.
He will join with them, only God knows when
God will place in their jaw that hook to draw
them down to the big event.

It seems that the stage is now being set
publicly on television.
Defiantly, masked men are cutting of heads,
goading the west to the battle ahead
that they see in their twisted vision.

God portrays the event and reveals His intent
to rise up in His righteous wrath.
Pour out pestilence and blood
with a brimstone flood,
a consuming fiery bath.

God will turn them back, they will suffer the lack
of five parts, just a sixth will return.
Israel will rejoice and proclaim with one voice,
Jesus Christ their Messiah's alive, alive,
their God who helped them survive, survive,
as they saw their enemies burn.

Does God Know When I Sin

November 24, 2013

I have this recurring, unsettling thought
and I've talked about this before.
The I that I am is important to me,
not who I was, who I'm going to be,
don't we all feel that way, even more?

So where's the computer that tallies us up
but does also a great deal more.
That records if we're bad or we're
    now and then good,
keeping track of the things that
    we know we should
tidy up, if God's running the store.

It's apparently true that a record is kept,
at least that's what the bible says.
We will give an account for each idle word,
I don't know who records it but somebody heard,
do you think we should mend our ways?

By and large, I don't think that I've acted too bad,
here on earth with the path that I've trod.
If God's watching us here, from somewhere upstairs,
does He know what we think,
    or that everyone swears,
all have sinned, and come short of the glory of God.

I guess I'd be a fool if I didn't 'fess up,
and tell God I'm a sinful man.
'cause He knows anyways, in the bible it says,
that the wages of sin is the death man pays,
please Jesus, save me if You can.

About the Author

This picture was taken five years ago when I married the lovely Agnes Mary Martin...This was a second marriage for both of us as we both were widowed several years earlier...You can see my evident contentment in the picture, I had by now recovered from the loss of Margaret my first wife of fifty four years, as was Agnes Mary from her fifty year plus marriage... My birth date is Jan. 18, 1926 and Agnes Mary's is Jan 20, 1925, so close...A little quick math should tell you that she is now, in 2015, ninety years and I am eighty nine and closing fast...God has been good to us as we continue to enjoy our quiet married life together in fairly good health.

Born in Toronto, Canada in 1926, depression years...I later had stints in the R.C.A.F., Great Lakes shipping as fireman on a small coal burner, Canadian Army just before W.W.2 ended...Cast adrift after Army discharge, I worked at a number of forgettable jobs and then, through the intercession of my wife's uncle I became a retail clerk in a Brewers Warehousing Retail beer store...I became assistant manager and then manager and worked there for the next 27 years.

At fifty, I had a very intense Spiritual experience resulting in my resignation from the beer business... With my wife and younger daughter, we attended Youth With a Mission {YWAM} in Hawaii for six months, after which I worked at 100 Huntley St., Daily Christian Television in Toronto as head of Security Counselling Dept. for five years...My wife and I then moved to British Columbia to join our two married daughters where we continue to the present time... My first wife Margaret passed away and after a few years I met and married Agnes Mary, a lovely English lady I met in church, God is good.

Bob McCluskey